The buds at the top of the stem open last.

Pollen grains are made at the end of the stamens in anthers.

Thistle

Each flower has a bright pattern to attract bumblebees.

Wild pansy

Flowers

Written by David Burnie
Consultant: Mike Grant

DK

Penguin
Random
House

Senior editor Carrie Love
US Senior editors Margaret Parrish, Shannon Beatty
Assistant editor Prerna Grewal
Senior art editors Ann Cannings, Pallavi Narain
Project art editor Radhika Banerjee
Illustrators Abby Cook, Dan Crisp
Jacket coordinator Francesca Young
Jacket designers Dheeraj Arora, Suzena Sengupta
Senior DTP designer Jagtar Singh
DTP designer Dheeraj Singh

Picture researcher Sakshi Saluja
Producer, pre-production David Almond
Producer Basia Ossowska
Managing editors Laura Gilbert, Monica Saigal
Managing art editor Diane Peyton Jones
Deputy managing art editor Ivy Sengupta
Delhi team head Malavika Talukder
Art director Helen Senior
Publishing director Sarah Larter

Original edition
Project editor Christine Webb
Art editors Ch'en-Ling, Chris Legee
Senior editor Susan McKeever
Senior art editor Jacquie Gulliver
Production Catherine Semark
Photography by Roger Phillips
Editorial consultant David Sutton, The British Museum
(Natural History)

First American Edition, 1993
This edition published in the United States in 2019 by DK Publishing
345 Hudson Street, New York, New York 10014

A catalog record for this book
is available from the Library of Congress.
ISBN: 978-1-4654-7910-5

DK books are available at special discounts when purchased in bulk
for sales promotions, premiums, fund-raising, or educational use.
For details, contact: DK Publishing Special Markets, 345 Hudson Street, New York, New York 10014
SpecialSales@dk.com

Printed and bound in China

The publisher would like to thank the following for their kind permission to reproduce their photographs:
(Key: a-above; b-below/bottom; c-center; f-far; l-left; r-right; t-top)

4 Dreamstime.com: Elen33 (r); Voltan1 (br). **5 123RF.com**: Vasin Leenanuruksa. **8 123RF.com**: Teerayut Ninsiri (crb). **13 123RF.com**: Richard Griffi
(r). **Depositphotos Inc**: griffin024 (ca). **Dreamstime.com**: Whiskybottle (tr). **14 123RF.com**: Tamara Kulikova (b). **15 Dreamstime.com**: Firina (clb)
Romasph (br). **16–17 123RF.com**: Valerii Zan (b). **17 123RF.com**: Ihor Bondarenko (tl). **Dreamstime.com**: Sanja Baljkas (crb). **22 123RF.com**: Uliar
Dementieva (crb). **Dreamstime.com**: Marilyn Barbone (br). **25 Alamy Stock Photo**: Christian Musat (tr); Geoff Smith (crb). **Getty Images**: Martin Har
(cla). **Science Photo Library**: Dr. Jeremy Burgess (c). **26 Alamy Stock Photo**: Ahmed Jawid Asefi (clb). **27 Alamy Stock Photo**: blickwinkel (r).
28 123RF.com: serezniy (cl). **Dreamstime.com**: Katrina Brown / Tobkatrina (cr). **29 Dreamstime.com**: Kira Kaplinski / Kkaplin (tr). **30 Alamy Stoc
Photo**: blickwinkel (bl). **32 Dreamstime.com**: Sahua (bl). **33 123RF.com**: Ruttawee Jaigunta (cb); wiesdie (ca). **34 Depositphotos Inc**:
imagebrokermicrostock (r). **36 Dreamstime.com**: Andreevaee (r). **38 123RF.com**: PaylessImages (b). **39 Fotolia**: Zee (r). **41 Dreamstime.com**:
Andreykuzmin (Soil). **42 Alamy Stock Photo**: Dave Marsden (crb). **Dreamstime.com**: Simicv (bl). **43 123RF.com**: alekss (br); photoroad (tr);
Evgenyi Lastochkin (cr). **Alamy Stock Photo**: flowerphotos (bc). **Dreamstime.com**: Voltan1 (cla). **44 Dreamstime.com**: Marina Scurupii (fcr);
Svrid79 (cr). **123RF.com**: Iryna Khudoliy (tr). **Dreamstime.com**: Elen33 (cr). **47 Dreamstime.com**: Argenlant (cl). **48 123RF.com**: Teerayut
Yukuntapornpong (cr). **Depositphotos Inc**: belchonock (bl). **49 Dreamstime.com**: Alisali (tl); Ronnachai Limpakdeesavasd (r). **50 123RF.com**: volta
(r). **Dreamstime.com**: Antonel (bl). **50–51 123RF.com**: gromaler (b). **51 123RF.com**: Zdenek Precechtel (tr). **Dreamstime.com**: Christina Hudson (cl
52 Dreamstime.com: Iva Villi (cra). **53 123RF.com**: Vasin Leenanuruksa (b); zych (tr). **55 Depositphotos Inc**: ploutarxina (cl). **56 Getty Images**:
Eye Ubiquitous (cr). **57 123RF.com**: Rudmer Zwerver (tl). **Alamy Stock Photo**: Garden World Images Ltd (cb). **Depositphotos Inc**: PJ1960 (bl).
58 Dreamstime.com: Natador (cr)

Cover images: *Front*: **123RF.com**: Serezniy bl; **Alamy Stock Photo**: Christian Musat tr; **Dreamstime.com**: Firina tc, Svrid79 cra; **Fotolia**: Zee c; **Bac
Dreamstime.com**: Marilyn Barbone ca, Elen33 crb; *Spine*: **Dreamstime.com**: Irochka cb, Svrid79 bc

All other images © Dorling Kindersley
For further information see: www.dkimages.com

A WORLD OF IDEAS:
SEE ALL THERE IS TO KNOW
www.dk.com

Contents

Looking at flowers

It's hard to imagine a world without flowers. Plants that have flowers grow almost everywhere, from gardens to high mountains. Every flower has a particular shape and color, so that it can perform a special job. By the time you've finished reading this book, you'll know what this job is, and how the flower does it. Always ask permission before picking a flower.

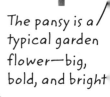

The pansy is a typical garden flower—big, bold, and bright

Animal visitors

Many flowers have lots of animal visitors throughout the day, or sometimes even at night. But what are these animals doing? Read on, and you'll find out.

This rose flower has a ring of five petals.

What's what?

There is much more to a flower than just its petals. Later on, you can discover what else makes up a flower, and what all the different parts do.

KEEPING A RECORD

Using colored pencils and a drawing pad, keep records of flowers that you see. A magnifying glass is useful for looking at flowers close-up; scissors and tweezers will help you to investigate the parts of a flower. A notebook is the flower explorer's most important piece of equipment. If you want a lasting reminder of a flower's shape, you can learn how to press it.

⚠️ Be careful while using scissors. Always ask an adult to help.

Drawing flowers helps you to see how the different parts fit together.

Making seeds

Once a flower has withered, it starts to make seeds. Some seeds come in juicy cases. We call them fruit. Later on, you will see how seeds are scattered, and how they turn into new plants.

A cherry is a juicy fruit that contains a single seed.

Flowers in close-up

A good way to find out about flowers is to take one apart. The petals are often big and bright. If you take the petals off, however, you will be left with the important parts of a flower—the ones that make the seeds.

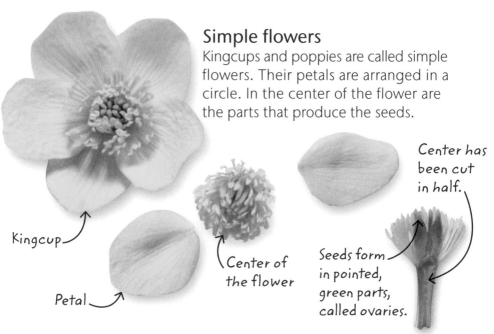

Simple flowers
Kingcups and poppies are called simple flowers. Their petals are arranged in a circle. In the center of the flower are the parts that produce the seeds.

Center has been cut in half.

Kingcup

Petal

Center of the flower

Seeds form in pointed, green parts, called ovaries.

Zoom in
Use a magnifying glass to look more closely at flowers. This will give you a better view of the different parts.

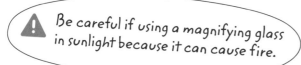

Be careful if using a magnifying glass in sunlight because it can cause fire.

Many flowers in one

From a distance, this thistle seems like a single flower, but take a closer look. It is made of many tiny flowers, called florets, packed together. In the daisy's "face," you will see lots of tiny dots. Each of these is a tiny flower. Flowers, such as thistles and daisies, are composite flowers.

Thistle

Each strand is a flower.

Tufty thistle

Look around in your yard or in the park, and see how many composite flowers you can spot. The tiny florets of this thistle make a tuft that looks like a bush.

Inside the thistle, you can see the tubelike florets.

Daisy pieces

Pull apart a large daisy to see the different florets that make it up. Each floret makes a single seed.

The "face" is made up of many tiny florets.

Each petal is really a separate, lopsided flower.

Complicated flowers

If you look at flowers in a garden or in the countryside, you will see that they come in many shapes. Some flowers are flat and round. Others are shaped like funnels, beaks, or even umbrellas. These types of flowers are called complicated flowers.

How many petals?

An everlasting pea has five petals. Two are joined together making the inside of the "beak," which sticks forward. Two more lie on either side, while the fifth makes a curved "hood" around the top of the flower.

The "beak" is made up of four petals.

Try and guess how many flowers a flower head has in this picture, and then count them.

"Hood" petal

"Beak" petal

"Beak" petal

Anthers hold a yellow dust called pollen.

Growing together

Many complicated flowers grow together in clusters, called flower heads.

Piped aboard

The Dutchman's-pipe plant has flowers that look just like a pipe. They attract flies with their sickly smell. The flies can only escape when stiff hairs inside the flower wither.

A living trap

Imagine being caught in a trap, dusted with pollen, and then released. That is what happens to tiny flies that visit the lords-and-ladies plant.

Spadix

Flies tumble from the spadix, or hood, into a lower chamber, which contains tiny flowers.

The club-shaped spadix gives off a scent that attracts tiny flies.

The hood has a slippery lining.

Lower chamber

Flowers with a difference

In nature, things are not always what they seem. Some plants have small, drab flowers, but they still manage to put on a brilliant show of color. Instead of petals, they use brightly colored leaves, or sepals, to attract insects.

Find that flower!
Most of this sun-spurge flower head is made up of special cup-shaped leaves, called bracts. The flowers themselves are tiny, and they nestle in the middle of each cup.

Two in one
Take a look at this "lacecap" hydrangea flower head. It is made up of many tightly packed flowers. Some of the flowers have big, colorful sepals, while the others are very small.

Inner flowers are much smaller. Only these can make seeds.

Outer flowers have four big, colorful sepals to attract insects.

Tropical treat

You have to look closely to see this plant's true flowers, because they are small. The flowers are surrounded by special pink leaves. The plant's name, bougainvillea (*boo-gan-vil-ia*), is quite a mouthful!

Flower

This colored leaf is called a bract.

Bougainvillea is a climbing plant.

Ordinary leaf

Leaf stems cling on by hooking around other plants.

Showy sepals

The showy flower of this clematis is actually a ring of sepals. Many plants have small green sepals, but the clematis has sepals that are bigger and more colorful than the rest of the flower.

Sepals

Colorful leaves

When growing wild, poinsettia (*poyn-set-ee-ah*) plants grow into big bushes, topped by leaves that turn crimson during the flowering season. The poinsettia's real flowers are surrounded by these bright leaves.

15

Plants that don't flower

No matter how well you look after a fern, you will never persuade it to flower. Nor will you ever see flowers on a moss. This is because moss doesn't have flowers or seeds. Instead, moss reproduces by making dust-like spores.

Tree ferns have thick "trunks." Some grow as high as a house.

Feathery ferns

Most ferns live in damp places. Their leaves, or fronds, are often split into many pieces, giving them a feathery outline. An easy way to spot ferns is to look at their new fronds. These usually have a coiled shape, which unwinds as they grow bigger.

Many ferns carry their spores on the back of fronds.

Slime and seaweed

In summer, ponds sometimes fill with green slime. This is made up of tiny algae—very simple plants that have no flowers. There are thousands of kinds of algae, including seaweed, and the green "dust" that covers tree trunks.

Slow, but sure

Look carefully at rocks, walls, and tree trunks for lichens. They look like flat patches that have been stuck on. They grow very slowly, but live for a long time. Lichens are only half plant, since they are a mix of fungus and alga.

Some lichens are brightly colored.

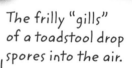

A lichen expands outward as it grows.

The frilly "gills" of a toadstool drop spores into the air.

Wet and dry

Mosses are small plants that usually live in damp places. Some live on walls and rooftops, where it can get very dry. In hot weather, they turn gray and hard. When it rains, they turn green and start growing again.

Mushrooms and toadstools

Most fungi feed on the remains of other living things. A mushroom or a toadstool is just the part of a fungus that makes spores. The rest of the fungus is hidden away. Although fungi look like plants, they aren't.

The life of a flower

Have you ever noticed how wild poppies can suddenly spring up on a patch of bare ground? This happens because most poppies are "annual" plants. They grow very quickly, and they flower and die all within the space of a year. Not all plants are like this. Many more live for a number of years. Plants like this are called "perennials" (*per-en-ee-als*).

The poppy is fully open.

Poppy flower folded up inside bud

Flower bud

Rushing into flower

The poppy is an annual plant. It puts all its energy into flowering and making lots of seeds as quickly as it can. A single poppy flower can make hundreds of seeds.

Long-lived plants

These garden cranesbills are perennials. They have big leaves and spreading roots. The leaves die in the fall, but the roots stay alive through the winter. In the spring, new leaves grow and cranesbills flower once again.

The poppy petals start to wither and fall off.

Perennial plants grow where the ground is not disturbed, from woodlands to deserts.

A single cranesbill flower makes just five seeds.

Annual plants like this poppy grow best where the soil has been dug, plowed, or moved around.

Seeds are shaken out by the wind. The cycle begins again the next year, when the seeds germinate.

Seeds are made in this chamber.

Chamber containing seeds

Bursting into flower

A flower bud is like a well-packed suitcase. It has a tough outer cover, which stops it from being damaged. Inside, the different parts of the flower are rolled up tight, so they take up very little space. As the bud grows, the flower expands inside. Soon, the flower becomes so big that it can no longer fit in the bud. Then it bursts into bloom.

The highest bud flowers first. When it withers, the next bud opens.

Petals unfold after bursting through the bud's papery sepals.

Iris flower buds grow out from folds in the pointed leaves.

The buds are protected by sepals.

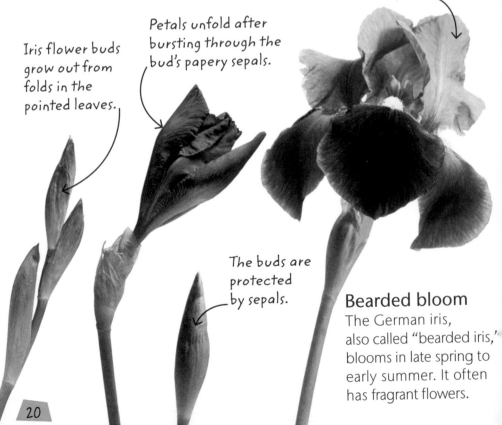

Bearded bloom
The German iris, also called "bearded iris," blooms in late spring to early summer. It often has fragrant flowers.

The three petals of an iris that point upward are called the "standards." In this iris, they are frilly and rounded. →

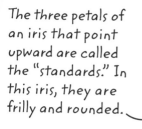

Calling all bees
An iris is not just a pretty shape—it is a complicated machine that attracts bees to visit it. Once a bee has landed, the flower sprinkles it with a dust called pollen.

The three drooping petals are called "falls."

Bees use falls as landing platforms.

Streaks on the petals guide bees to a sweet food called nectar at the center of the flower.

Pretty in pink
This lily bud is shaped like a torpedo. It has six long, pointed petals. Lilies grow from bulbs and come in a range of colors.

Anther coated with pollen

Tightly rolled petals

Ovary

Inside the bud
This iris bud has been sliced open just before it was about to bloom. See if you can make out the rolled-up petals and the ovary, where the seeds are made.

Blooming colors

Flowers use their colors to attract insects. When a bee or a butterfly sees a brightly colored flower, it flies toward it. The color is like a signpost that shows where tasty nectar can be found.

Color pigments
Flowers contain natural substances called pigments, which give color to their petals. The varying colors are a result of the different types of pigment present.

Dyes from plants
Ancient Greeks and Romans used plant pigments to dye their clothes. They used crocus flowers to make yellow, woad plant to make blue, and the roots of madder plants for red.

Crocus flower

Madder roots

Woad plant

DO-IT-YOURSELF COLORS

To see how a flower draws up water, you will need some white carnation flowers, tap water, and food coloring.

1. Take a white carnation and ask an adult to split the lower half of the stem in two.

3. Within an hour, one half will change color! This happens because the flower draws up the water and the color through the stem.

2. Put one side in tap water, and the other in water with food coloring.

Water with food coloring

Tap water

Green for growth

Plants have a green pigment in their leaves called chlorophyll. Chlorophyll is very important for plants, because it collects energy from sunlight so that they can grow. Before their leaves drop, the green color of the leaves changes into yellow and red—the colors you see in the fall.

All about pollen

Every living thing on Earth is made up of tiny parts, called cells. A plant cannot grow until two kinds of cell join together. One kind of cell is called an ovule. Ovules are formed in the base of the flower, inside a chamber called an ovary. The other kind of cell is called a pollen grain. Pollen grains are tiny. They have to join up with the ovules from another flower, so they have to move from one flower to another.

Stamen

Coming and going

This lily flower makes ovules as well as pollen grains. However, it will only form seeds if it receives pollen that has traveled from another lily flower.

The stigma is a landing platform that receives pollen from other flowers.

The pollen grains are made at the end of the stamens in anthers.

A pollen grain lands on the stigma and grows a tube to the ovary.

Stigma

A seed is formed here, in the ovary.

Pollen at the ready
This lily bud has been cut in half to reveal its stamens and stigma. At the end of each stamen is a dark orange anther. This makes the pollen, which is like a fine dust.

Pollen in close-up
Pollen grains are so small that about 50 of them can fit on a pinhead. Every plant has its own type of pollen. Some are round, while others are shaped like triangles or sausages.

Magnified pollen grain of a hollyhock

Spikes

Hollyhock plant

Anther

A single anther makes millions of pollen grains.

Sticky business
Pollen grains are often sticky. When a bee visits a flower, it cannot keep from brushing against the anthers and getting covered in pollen.

Animal visitors

Have you ever noticed insects flitting from flower to flower? They are spreading pollen. When a bee visits a flower, it gets dusted with pollen. When it moves on to another flower, it unloads some of the pollen and picks up some more. In return for its hard work, the bee gets "paid" with sugary nectar.

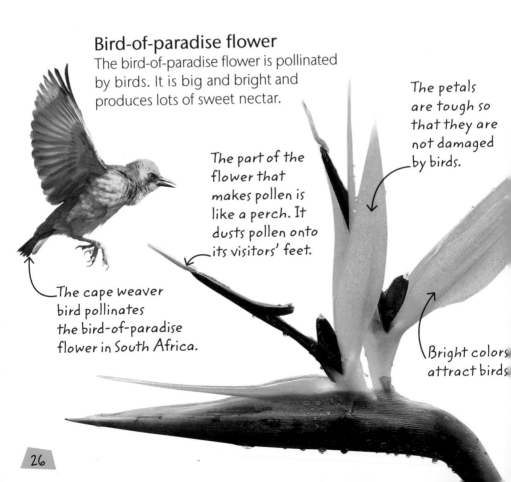

Bird-of-paradise flower
The bird-of-paradise flower is pollinated by birds. It is big and bright and produces lots of sweet nectar.

The petals are tough so that they are not damaged by birds.

The part of the flower that makes pollen is like a perch. It dusts pollen onto its visitors' feet.

The cape weaver bird pollinates the bird-of-paradise flower in South Africa.

Bright colors attract birds

A face full of pollen

Wild fuchsias (*few-shas*) are often visited by hummingbirds. As the hummingbird hovers to drink the nectar, its face gets dusted with pollen. It then carries the pollen to the next flower it visits.

Hummingbirds usually visit red flowers.

Painted lady butterfly

Long stamens dust the hummingbird with pollen.

Teasel flowers have lots of nectar.

Prickly drink

The teasel is preferred by insects with long tongues. Butterflies and bumblebees can reach past the teasel's long spikes to drink its nectar, but ordinary honeybees cannot reach far enough.

Look for seed-eating birds near teasel plants. They love to eat teasel seeds.

27

Perfumed flowers

Have you ever wondered why flowers smell? The answer isn't to please our noses. Instead, flowers use smell as a signal. Their scent spreads into the air, where bees and other insects can detect it. The insects fly to where the scent is strongest. This leads them to the flowers, and to a sugary meal. Most flowers smell strongest by day, but a few release more of their scent at night.

Freesia flowers open one after the other. Each flower lasts for several days.

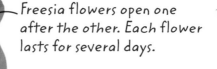

Bees are attracted to flowers with a sweet smell and bright colors.

Sweet-smelling freesias

Freesia flowers produce a rich scent for many days, which is why they are often cut and brought indoors. Twenty kinds of freesia grow in the wild, but many more varieties have been specially bred by gardeners.

Bell-shaped flowers

Calling all bees

Grape hyacinths have small, bell-shaped flowers. They give off a rich scent during the day, attracting bees in early spring. Grape hyacinths can often be found in parks and gardens.

A scent in the night

Try this: smell a honeysuckle's flowers during the day and then in the evening. You will find that the evening scent is much stronger. Honeysuckle is pollinated mainly by moths. It releases its perfume after dark to attract its nighttime visitors.

Smelly monster
The world's biggest flower is the giant Rafflesia. It grows up to 31 in (80 cm) across and attracts flies by smelling like rotting meat!

Moths have long tongues that can reach deep into the honeysuckle's tubelike flowers.

The evening primrose has a strong scent and pale color to guide moths toward it.

Night shift
Many flowers open up during the day and close at night. The flowers of evening primrose work the other way around. As dusk falls, they open wide and release their scent to attract moths.

Floating in the wind

Not all flowers are pollinated by animals. Instead, some use the wind. These types of flower shed their pollen into the air, and the tiny grains are blown far and wide. Some pollen lands on the ground, some gets in our eyes and noses, and just enough lands on other flowers. If you suffer from hay fever, you may know all about this.

Stand back!
Stinging nettle flowers shed their pollen into the air in a special way. When the pollen grains are ripe, a tiny "explosion" in each flower shoots the pollen into the air.

Afloat in a boat
A few plants use water to move their pollen. This is Canadian pondweed, a plant that you might see in fish tanks. It has two different kinds of flower, both on long stalks that reach up to the surface. The male flowers scatter their pollen over the water. Each pollen grain drifts until it pollinates a female flower.

Blooming unnoticed

Grasses have flowers, too, but their flowers are often small and dull. Many are surrounded by green scales, making them difficult to spot. Like all wind-pollinated flowers, grasses do not need bright petals to attract insects. Their flowers grow in clusters at the top of tall stems. Next time you walk through a field of long grass, watch out for puffs of pollen as you brush against them.

People who suffer from hay fever are allergic to pollen. They suffer most in spring and early summer, when grasses release lots of pollen into the air.

Bearded wheat

Barley

Grasses such as this Timothy shed their pollen into the air, where it is spread by the wind.

Wild oat

Like grasses, plantain has tiny flowers packed together on top of a long stem.

Seed story

Seeds come in all shapes and sizes. Some are as big as a soccer ball. Others are so small that millions can fit inside a matchbox. When the seeds are ready, they leave the parent plant and begin a new life on their own. Some seeds drop to the ground, but more often they scatter far and wide.

No seeds

Not all plants produce seeds. The baby pick-a-back plant grows from the parent plant's leaf. It grows out from where the stalk joins the leaf. When the parent plant bends over and touches the ground, the baby plant takes root.

Dandelion flower

Flyaway seeds

If you blow hard on a dandelion's seeds, they fly away. Each seed has a tiny parachute to help it float in the air. This helps the wind blow the seeds a very long way, so they can take root on a new patch of ground.

...re lovers

...anksias grow in the dry bush of ...ustralia. Their hard, wooden seed ...ods stay tightly shut until a fire ...weeps through the bush. When the ...re is over, the seed pods open up, ...nd the seeds drop onto the ground.

Seed head

...owers ...ither and ...op off when ...eds form.

Hard pod containing a seed

...andle with care

...astor oil seeds contain ...deadly poison. However, ...hen they are crushed, ...e seeds produce ...valuable oil, which ...used as a medicine.

Seeds grow inside a spiny case.

Castor oil seeds

Burdock seed head

Taken for a ride

If you go for a walk in the country, seeds often stick to your clothes. This is how burdock seeds spread— by "hitching a ride" with passing animals and people.

Juicy fruits

Have you ever wondered why some plants pack up their seeds in such a juicy way? The answer is that it helps them to spread. When a bird feeds on berries, it swallows the fruit, complete with the seeds. The seeds pass straight through its body and out with its droppings. They land on the ground and sprout, often far from the plant that produced them.

The story of a strawberry

Wild strawberries are small, and it takes a lot to make a mouthful. Garden strawberries have been made bigger by "crossing" different kinds of wild strawberry and by growing only the plants that give the biggest, sweetest fruit.

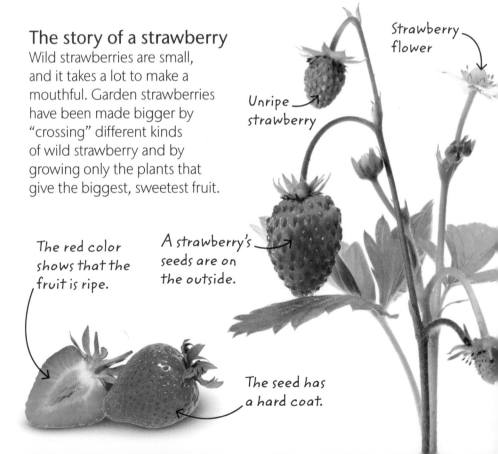

Strawberry flower

Unripe strawberry

A strawberry's seeds are on the outside.

The red color shows that the fruit is ripe.

The seed has a hard coat.

Known by name

Apples have been grown for so long that there are now many different varieties to choose from. Each variety has its own name. This apple is a Red Delicious.

Seeds

Apple blossom

After an apple flower is pollinated, the base of the flower swells up around the seeds to make the fruit, which is the apple.

An apple's seeds are surrounded by the thick, juicy flesh.

Flowers and seeds are hidden inside the fig.

The fig's hidden secret

No matter how much you search, you will never see blossom on a fig tree. This is because each fig is filled with hundreds of tiny flowers.

Figs are pollinated by a tiny female wasp. It squeezes through a hole in the end of the fig and spreads pollen over the flowers inside.

What do a tomato, a cucumber, and a pod full of peas have in common? You may think they are vegetables, but, strictly speaking, they are fruits, because they all contain seeds.

35

Flowers from bulbs

Next time you see someone slicing open an onion, ask if you can have a closer look. (This might make your eyes water!) You will see that the onion is made up of many tightly packed layers. Onions are bulbs, just like tulips and daffodils. Each layer of a bulb is a pantry for food. This food is used up as the plant grows.

When you go for a walk in spring, see if you can guess which flowers grow from bulbs.

This parrot tulip's frilly, curled petals look like a parrot's feathers.

Fit for a prince
Wild tulips grow in hot countries such as Turkey. Hundreds of years ago, Turkish princes grew them around their palaces. Today, many kinds of tulips are grown all over the world.

Daffodil

Narcissus

Hyacinth

Fritillary

Crocus

WATCHING A BULB GROW

Sit a hyacinth bulb on a glass jar or vase. Fill the jar with water and make sure that the bottom of the bulb just touches the water. Roots and leaves will soon appear, followed by the flower. When the flower withers, plant the bulb in soil. This lets it make more food reserves so it can flower again next year.

The hyacinth bulb is packed full of food reserves.

South American giant

Hippeastrums (*hippy-as-trums*) grow wild in the mountain forests of South America. However, you don't have to clamber through a tropical forest to see these giants—they will flower quite happily on your windowsill.

Huge flowers shaped like trumpets

Sliced open, the bulb shows many closely packed layers.

Roots

The strong, hollow stem is about 30 in (75 cm) tall. It holds the flower up above the leaves. Each stem bears between three and six flowers.

37

Springing into life

Seeds may look dry and dead, but inside each one are living cells waiting for the chance to divide and grow. The wait may be a long one, from weeks to months to years. As soon as it is damp enough and warm enough, however, the seed's cells start to divide, and a new plant comes to life. This is called germination.

First steps

Like most seeds, the sunflower germinates root first so that it can take in water from the soil. The stem then appears at the other end, and as it grows longer it lifts the seed's hard case off the ground. Eventually, the case splits and falls off.

Seed case fall off to reveal two rounded seed leaves.

The stem becomes longer.

Seed

A green stem appears.

The root grows downward.

Striking oil

About one-third of a sunflower seed's weight is made up of oil. You may have seen sunflower oil in your kitchen—it is often used in cooking and for making margarine.

A treat for the birds

Most sunflowers are annual plants, which means that they germinate, flower, and die in the same year. Although they live for just a few months, they can get very large. If you grow a sunflower, don't cut it down after it has finished flowering. Instead, leave it and watch the birds arrive to feast on its seeds.

A sunflower's face always points toward the sun.

"Giant" sunflower plants may grow to more than 10 ft (3 m) high.

If you plant seeds of a "giant" variety of sunflower, your plant may grow taller than you!

39

A flying start

A single plant can make hundreds or even thousands of seeds. Each seed contains a food supply. When a seed germinates, the young plant uses this food supply to help it through its first few days of life.

Racing ahead

Pole bean seeds are fun to grow because they get off to a flying start. This is because each fat seed has a large food supply packed into two special seed leaves. In some plants, such as the sunflower, the seed leaves open out above the ground. However, in the pole bean, they stay below the surface.

A second pair of leaves opens out.

The stem grows longe

The leaves get bigger.

Hooked shoot grows upward through the ground.

Shoot straightens out above the ground.

First leaves open.

Seed leav shrink as food supp is used u

Root grows out of a split in the seed case.

AMAZING BEAN!

When a plant germinates, it grows toward the light. You can see this for yourself by growing a bean in a shoebox "maze." You will need a bean, a plant pot, soil, tape, and a pair of scissors.

⚠️ Be careful while using scissors. Always ask an adult to help.

1. Cut a window in one end of the box, and then make two cardboard shelves that stick out from the sides. Stand the box on end.

2. Now plant a bean in a pot, put the pot inside, and put the lid tightly on the box. When the bean germinates, it will find its way through the maze and out of the window! Remember to water the bean as it grows.

Window

Shelf

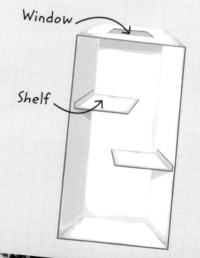

The plant grows around the shelf in its search for light.

Position the bean in the middle of the soil.

Garden flowers

Have you ever noticed that some garden flowers look very much like wild ones, but are bigger and brighter? The reason for this is that all garden plants originally came from the wild. They look different now because gardeners, not nature, decide which plants to breed.

Putting on a show

Like many garden plants, these polyanthuses are hybrids. This means that their wild ancestors were not polyanthuses at all, but different plants. The wild primrose is just one of the polyanthus's distant ancestors.

Look for wild primroses growing in shady hedgerows and at the edge of woodlands.

Garden pansy

Wild pansy

The queen of flowers

Roses have been grown for thousands of years. Most garden roses are much bigger than their wild relatives. They can keep flowering for months, rather than just a few weeks.

Garden roses often have many petals.

Wild roses have just five petals.

Flowers with a face

Wild and garden pansies both have flat flowers that look like faces. If you look closely, you'll see that the face is made up of five petals. The garden pansy has bigger petals that overlap.

Sowing themselves

Wild poppies live all over the world, from the Arctic to the tropics. Garden poppies are easy to grow, and new plants often spring up year after year.

Garden poppy

Wild poppy

Making flowers last

Most flowers last for a few days, but some last just a single morning. By pressing or drying flowers, you can make them last far longer. Pressing a flower keeps the outline of its shape, while drying it helps to keep its scent.

PRESSING FLOWERS

Place a sheet of thick blotting paper in a book. Spread the flowers out on the paper, then cover them with another sheet and close the book. Now stack some heavy books on top. Wait at least a week before carefully peeling away the paper to see the pressed flowers.

Pressing works best with small or papery flowers, such as pansies and poppies.

People often use flower to mark special occasion In Hawaii, a flower garland, or lei, is a way of saying "welcome."

MAKING POTPOURRI

Potpourri (po-pour-ee) is a colorful mixture of small, scented flowers and petals. To make potpourri, you will need a baking sheet and some flowers.

1. Pick the flowers when the weather is warm and dry. Leave the small flowers whole, but pull the petals off the large flowers one by one.

2. Lay the flowers and petals on the sheet, spreading them out to make a thin layer.

3. Every day, move the petals around so that the air dries them evenly. The mixture is ready when it rustles when you stir it. This usually takes at least a week.

4. Put the finished mixture in a bowl, so that the potpourri fills a room with its scent.

Woodland flowers

With so many trees, woods are mostly dark. When the trees shed their leaves, however, plants get enough light to flower. The plants flower in spring and try to make the most of the light before the trees bear leaves again.

The buds at the top of the stem open last.

Each flower has a bright pattern to attract bumblebees.

Going up

The foxglove grows in woodland clearings. It has dozens of flowers that sprout from its tall stem. If you look closely, you can often see bumblebees clambering around inside the flowers.

Scented lily

Lily of the valley has tiny, bell-shaped flowers that give off a rich scent. In the wild, it grows in dry woodlands.

Wild garlic

Wild garlic carpets woodland floors in spring. It is also commonly known as ramson. The plant has a strong smell of garlic and all its parts can be eaten.

The flowers are star-shaped and have six petals.

Leafless flower stalk.

Closing time

Wood sorrel grows in woods and on shady banks. Its leaves have three parts, called leaflets. The leaflets close up at night. They look a bit like folded umbrellas.

Leaflet

Spring flowers

Bluebells flower in the middle of spring, just as the trees around them begin to sprout their leaves.

Tropical flowers

In many parts of the world, plants stop growing during winter. In the tropics, however, particularly where it is wet, they can grow and flower all year round. You don't have to go to the tropics to see flowers like these, because in cooler places they are often grown as indoor plants.

Threatened orchids

Orchids grow all over the world, but the biggest and most spectacular live in the tropics. Some kinds have become very rare because too many have been collected and sold.

Insects land on the flower's tail and pollinate it.

Brilliant scarlet hood attracts insects.

Paphiopedilum (paf-ee-o-ped-i-lum) orchids come from Southeast Asia.

The tail flower

Wild tail flowers grow in the forests of South America, but they are popular indoor plants. See how many different-colored tail flowers you can spot.

Shiny leaves stay green all year round.

Passionflower

Passionflowers climb up other plants and hang on by their curly tendrils. Their flowers are visited by bees and hummingbirds, and each one lasts for just a single day.

Plant piggyback

In a tropical forest, the place to look for orchids is often not on the ground, but high up in the trees. Many orchids live by "perching" on branches or tree trunks. They don't do any harm to the trees. However, by being higher up, they do get a better share of the daylight.

Orchids can also be grown as houseplants.

Grassland flowers

In days gone by, fields and open grassy spaces were often full of wild flowers. However, after tractors and weedkillers were invented, many wild flowers were plowed up, or killed by poisonous sprays. Grassland flowers still survive, but in special places. Look for them in old pastures, on roadsides, around the edges of fields, and on steep banks and slopes.

Nodding bells
The harebell's light blue flowers look like tiny bells as they nod in the wind. Harebells thrive in rough pastures where the soil is shallow.

Harebell flowers grow on long, thin stalks.

Holding its ground
Yarrow is a very tough grassland plant. It can survive being cut by a lawnmower, and it even thrives by the sides of roads.

Seeds that stick

If you walk through a field where agrimony has just finished flowering, you may help it to spread. Agrimony's hooked seeds will cling to your clothes if you brush past them.

The prairies of North America used to be filled with wild flowers. When the prairies were turned into farmland, many wild flowers disappeared.

Agrimony flowers grow on a long stem.

From prairie to garden

Coneflowers get their name because their petals point slightly downward, giving the flowers a pointed shape. Coneflowers are often grown in gardens—look for their flowers in late summer.

Yarrow and poppies in a field

51

Waterside flowers

The banks of many lakes and streams are like watery jungles—packed with plants and flowers. You'll find that water and marsh plants are choosy about where they grow. Some need ground that is damp, but not too wet. Other plants grow in the water, but are rooted to the bottom. A few just float on the surface, with their roots trailing in the water.

At the water's edge

If you look at the water's edge, you can see how different plants grow in different places. However, make sure that an adult is watching when you are exploring near water.

Monkey flower

Look for the monkey flower on the banks o streams. You can see it: bright yellow flowers i late summer.

Reed mace (or cattail) grows in the water. Its flower head looks just like a sausage.

Meadowsweet's creamy colored flowers have a rich scent. Look for meadowsweet by the banks of streams.

Hemp agrimony grows in damp ground. It has small, tube-shaped flowers in big clusters.